The 24 Hours Before

Best of life

Andy Marquez

Copyright 2012

"Dawn of the Cenazoic"

Introduction

I did not even have the idea for this book until late in 2011. A customer asked me the question "How long did you have to wait to take this picture?" He was talking about one of my Canyonlands photos, "Dawn of the Cenazoic". This made me think about all that actually goes into taking a shot. On this occasion, I'd been there before, when I photographed "Warning of the Washer Woman" back in 1989. I knew I could sleep in Moab, get up at 5, drive the thirty-four miles to the Mesa Arch trailhead, hike the ½ mile down to the arch and be ready to shoot before sunrise. In this particular case, I was there about 10 minutes before.

The actual wait time at the scene is really insignificant compared to, in many cases, the planning. On overseas and a lot of U.S. trips, there's a fair amount of research that goes into it, before you actually set the sails in motion. Where do I want to shoot? Where should I stay? How do I get there? What's it going to cost? When is the best time to go? Can I do this alone? Can Teresa go with me, if not her, maybe one of the kids? Perhaps, a friend? The pictures themselves tell a part of the story. The moments before can be glorious, as the light changes before my very eyes. So I thought it would be interesting to write about what's gone on for the past 24 hours, before I actually clicked the shutter. Some of the images were planned, others just happened.

In the case of this Canyonlands shot, it was just of day of driving from Roxborough to Moab, and spending the next morning in this Utah National Park. But for many other images, it was a far different story. I've gone back in time to relive the 24 hours before 24 separate shots were taken. Here you will find those recollections, some of the words are from diaries, while others are from my wonderful memories.

"The Sacred Season"
Taos, New Mexico, April 1993

Having done some pretty decent snow pics over the years, there is one that eludes me, New Mexico's Taos Pueblo, in the snow. Here is the mission. It's 280 miles from home. I've tried this 4 previous times from chasing a storm too late from Santa Fe to Taos, or arriving and finding a closed pueblo. Decision time, it's supposed to snow in Taos the day after tomorrow. If we leave in the morning, we'll be ready when it comes and deal with getting back afterwards. We're going to do just that.

It's just past nine and we're headed down I-25 towards Walsenburg. The weather is partly cloudy and looking a little darker as we look to the south. Exiting the interstate, we head west on 160 over LaVeta Pass and down to Ft. Garland, where there is now a low ceiling of clouds. It's April 1st and it could rain or snow here, but nothing yet. We've turned south and are heading through San Luis into New Mexico, and guess what? Light snow begins to fall. Arriving 40 minutes later we pull into town and the weather has intensified! Now, the Taos Pueblo has to be open. And it is. We park our car by the old cemetery; quietly enter the pueblo, as the snow continues to fall. We pass St. Jerome's Chapel, their church built in 1876. And now I'm looking at the shot I've waited so long for. The time has finally come. This is for sure the Sacred Season.

"Eventide"
Santorini, Greece - October 1994

"Fasten you seatbelts and prepare for landing", the words that come over the loud speaker. I have a window seat and my half awake, Teresa, sits next to me. It has been a very long day and we are about to touch down on the island of Santorini in the Greek Isles. Close to midnight we arrive, and find our way to the Hotel Loucas located supposedly on the side of a cliff in Thira. Within 30 minutes we come to our accommodations, which we learned about in a guidebook. 200 plus steps we must go down to get to the check-in office. What a trek, carrying our luggage and camera gear. Entering our room, we become immediately aware of a puddle in the middle of the floor. A leaky roof. Too late to do anything about it now, I just want to sleep. 3 A.M., I awaken feeling shaky. It's low blood sugar and stupid as it may seem, I have nothing to eat or drink that will bring it up. I must go out, alone, up the stairs and find some sugar. A disco is nearby, but the music's too loud here and nobody speaks English. I wander the streets until close to 5 A.M., and

at last, find a diner. As I'm fading, I purchase a Coca Cola and somehow recovering, find my way back to the hotel, and my worried wife. Up and out at sunrise, we find a rust colored pot sitting on the edge of a whitewashed wall with the dark blue Agean Sea as background. My first overseas photograph. Later this morning, we are riding a bus to the ancient archeological site of Akotiri. Here we spend a couple of hours. Back to Thira. Before naptime, we decide to walk down to the port below. A local resident, leading a donkey, solicits us to ride. We decline. After a short rest, we hop aboard another bus and head toward Fira for a much talked about sunset. Not far off shore to the west, there is a smaller island that hosts a now silhouetted Greek Church. A very peaceful end to our first full day in a foreign country.

"Twilight Story"
Kenya, Africa - September 1995

It is within an hour of sunset on the plains of the Masai Mara. This will be our fourth night here. Francis, our guide, has spent the last few hours tracking down a white rhino, one of only five left in the park. We were successful in finding one, but the shot is what we call a "Hey, I'm a rhino" shot. No mood. Just before sunset, it seems Francis knows the whereabouts of a handsome male lion. Lo and behold, we pull up in the jeep close to him, his face badly scarred. I'm telling our guide, who has become our friend, the lion is in the "golden light". Back to the camp, excited about today's work in the field. I am still hoping to get the shot that says Africa all over it.

It is morning and we are meeting Francis to look for the one animal that has eluded us, the leopard. Teresa and I know that the minutes are dwindling away on our last day here. We are searching but cannot find the leopard, happy though to have seen the great wildebeest crossing the river. Mid afternoon has come and we feel something that we have not yet felt, the wind. It's beginning to really blow.

Now the sand is flying about. A very light rain begins to fall. Visibility is difficult. However, we can see a giraffe running with our jeep, a good forty yards away. Francis urges us to take our picture, because we may get stuck, as the ground is getting muddy. Yep, he's right, we are stuck! Here's my chance to run off seven shots of the giraffe running into the weather.

After note: Within thirty minutes two British blonde haired hunks come to our rescue, leaving us with a memory and a few photos never to forget.

"The Fridge"
Yellowstone, Wyoming - January 1995

The outside thermometer reads 8 degrees below zero. Mammoth Hot Springs in Wyoming's Yellowstone National Park is one of the few motels in the area that is open. It's the dead of winter, January, late morning. I'm here with my son, Chris, his friend Eric, and his dad, my friend Mark Kramer. We're about to board our rented snowmobiles, for this is the primo mode of transportation here this time of the year. I am seeing a lot of icicles hanging about. We're off, us, the two older gentlemen driving with our sons behind us. Today we're looking for whatever wildlife might cross our path. Bison, I already have featured in the shots "Homecoming" and "Old Man Winter". Sure would like a coyote shot. I've never captured one that I like. The temperature is struggling to get above zero. After a good 15 miles, Mark, who has taken the lead, the way he does things, slows down and points. There, not far off the road is a coyote. The falling snow creates minimal visibility. Using my 500 mm lens I get a close-up of the coyote's face, almost ghostly looking. Shortly after this, we encounter another coyote standing in the middle of the snow packed road. I'm thrilled. It's getting dark and we must return to the lodge by 4 P.M. We are back in time and chilled to the bone. Dinner and early to bed.

We begin our second day adventure earlier than yesterday. Within an hour we come upon a big bison, digging his face in the snow, his legs buried. The only problem here is he's kind of down this hill. But brave as we are, we get the camera gear and the four of us make our way down below. We're now within 30 feet of this great beast, as we stand in the white stuff a good six inches above our knees. No way to get away if he turns aggressive. The big ol' buffalo raises his snow-covered face and looks me in the eye. Click.

"Slumber Party"
Katmai, Alaska – September 1996

My two previous trips to Alaska were something this side of miserable. A 1989 trip to Kodiak Island was with a hired guide and a little group of five. Four fishermen and me, the solo photographer seeking out the Kodiak bear. Never did I see one. However, I guess I'm really lucky because I was left alone for two hours on the side of a riverbank with no protection, unaware of how dangerous this massive animal could be. A few years later, with the brother of a customer, I journeyed to Lake Illiama, where we found ourselves stranded on a little island, while continuous rain pounded us. The wind was whipping up, too rough to navigate our little boat back to the mainland. End result – we were okay, but once again, no bear photos.

These are the thoughts running through my brain, as my son, Chris, and I, head down to the river at Katmai National Park. Here we have been somewhat fortunate, we have seen a grizzly bear. On our first night here, we had a beautiful sunset and I captured it with a grizzly silhouetted in the foreground. It's been ugly cloudy since. What has eluded us is a pair of cubs, which we haven't been able to get within shootable distance of. Down at the river's edge, there's a platform that is usually crowded with photographers from all over the world, here to shoot these mighty animals. We have been hanging around for hours, there have been a few bear in the water, but the light has been crappy. We should head back to our cabin and get ready for our mess hall dinner, the last of the season on this September day. As we walk, there is a sudden disturbing sound. Running a few yards from us and passing at great speed are the two cubs, followed by Mama and then big Daddy. Quite a breathtaking moment.

We've come to the mess hall and they are serving shepherd's pie, made from all the leftovers of the past week. Tomorrow morning we will catch our little plane back to Anchorage. Night passes and it's time to go. We carry our bags to the plane. I'm going to check the beach one last time before leaving. There, lying in the sand, within appropriate distance from us, are our two cubs. One last shot, with a big smile.

"Magic Show"
Montreux, Switzerland - March 1999

"My hair is grey, but not with years, grew it white in a single night". The words of English poet Lord Byron, about a prisoner of the French Reformation, held captive in this castle we have visited tonight. We had arrived in Montreaux, on the Lake Geneva shoreline, earlier today on one of the always-on time Swiss trains. Bad weather in Zermatt provoked us to leave and spend an extra day here. Tomorrow morning we will return to the Chateau de Chillon, about three miles from the city center. Hoping dawn will bring a clear day so we can see the French Alps, across the lake.

Chris and I are up early, taking a bus to the castle. There has not been much of a sunrise, however there is quite a haze in the air. You can't tell where the water meets the sky. As we arrive at the castle, I realize this could be an interesting shot. Its now just past 8 A.M. and we've gone into the castle, now that it's open to the public. Inside the walls and through a cobblestone courtyard. We are now entering a huge room with big pillars and sculptured archways. This is where Byron came to visit the prisoner. I'm lost for words, a flash back in time. It's about one man's freedom. Exploring more of the castle, through passageways, we come upon an old wooden door that opens to the lake, however bars block any escape. The lake water has turned a turquoise color. Enjoying the mid day and afternoon, meandering through the castle. We have come to Switzerland to photograph the magnificent Alps, however have found a new direction in this Chateau de Chillon. Spending most of the daylight hours here, it's time to head back. There is a walking path that runs along the side of the lake back to Montreaux center. We are following it, a beautiful way to return to our hotel as we watch the sun setting. I pause and get the camera out for another image from this day. It is still quite hazy. The ball of the sun is red with a yellow core. It appears to be balancing on the fingers of a tree branch. A magic show.

"Tunnel Vision"
Burano, Italy - October 1997

Grandma's two bags, T's big suitcase, my big suitcase, Chris' smaller one, Leanne's even smaller one, Nikki's diaper bag, two tripods and two camera bags, my "Uncle Onion" shoulder bag, oh yes – Nikki and the stroller! This is what we are unloading off the vaparetto to our hotel room on Lido. We settle and are ready for dinner. Nothing, but good ol' Italian pizza for dinner, will do. Each slice has come with a single sunny side up egg on the cheese. This is Grandma's 75th birthday trip, her first time overseas, so we decided, why not bring the whole family. On all previous trips, I've had only one person with me. So far, so good. Tomorrow we'll be in Venice, I can't believe it. Soon we'll get some sleep following a difficult day of travel. Upon hitting the sack, I feel like I nearly hit the floor. Good Lord, these beds are way soft. I'm struggling to find comfort, there's only one way- to sleep on the floor!

Morning has brought us back to the island of Venice, and to San Marco Plaza. A magnificent church. The angels on the steeple are backlit. The kids and grandma are feeding the huge amount of pigeons that are surrounding us. We have played for an hour or so, and it's very crowded here, impossible to set up a tripod. The island of Burano, where color rules, is just a 45 minute vaparetto ride away. Onward! As we approach the shoreline, we can see the brightly colored houses becoming vibrant. Now that we have docked, I know there is limited time that we have before the sun falls below a cloudbank in the west. It's 3 P.M. Chris and I hustle ahead toward a canal we saw coming in. A little confusing here, trying to find the way through passageways unknown. Teresa, Leanne, Grandma and little Nikki in the stroller, are way behind us. Turning one corner, I stop dead in my tracks. We are in what seems like a tunnel with peach, red and green walls, and at the end, is what jammed on the breaks. As we're setting up the camera, a brightly illuminated blue door mesmerizes me, with a blue and white curtain, blowing in the wind.

"The Lost City"
Machu Picchu, Peru ~ May 1998

I am sitting here in a popular restaurant on the square in downtown Cusco, 10,000 feet up in the Andes Mountains. With me is a close friend, good ol' Gilbert. While doing an art show at Cinderella City Mall in 1987, he bought a framed copy of my buffalo picture "Homecoming". We became buds. He soon was our insurance agent, and did some dry wall work for us at our gallery. It's been said he built many walls. Am I failing to mention that Gilbert paid for a run of 8x10 lithos of my horse picture "Frosty Noses"? His dad financed a run of 6 posters, 1,000 copies each. And now he's accompanying me to this third world country, Peru. Some other friends from Denver are in Cusco on their return from Machu Picchu. Having dinner with Alex and Laurie, we soon find out that guinea pig is the gourmet dish here. No thanks; we'll take the beef. We're returning to our hotel room to get ready for tomorrow's journey to the Lost City. The water is not working, not from the faucet nor the toilet. Just lovely. Management says they're working on it, perhaps by 3 A.M. Our alarms go off just past 4 A.M. and who would have believed it, there is still no water. I'll skip the details. Off we go, aboard kind of an old train headed for the Inca Ruins of Machu Picchu. The train ride is very bumpy, riding with the chickens. I'm becoming nauseated, but the incredible views of 20,000 foot mountain peaks are comforting. Early afternoon we arrive at the village of Aquas Caliente, where we transfer to a bus that goes up the hill to our $192 a night stay at the Machu Picchu Hotel. We're here for just one. Not much time to come up with a shot. There's a young boy who keeps cutting across the switchbacks in front of the bus, and upon reaching the top, his hand is out for tips. Funny. We check in and Gilbert manages to talk me into paying $59 each to have a helicopter return us to Cusco.

We've hired a guide, Francisco, who is taking us through the ancient entrance and on an upward hike to where the 26 mile Inca Trail comes to an end. Along the way we're finding little white caterpillars, too small to even photograph without a macro lens.

We begin to head back down. As the sun descends in the sky, we come to The Temple of the Sun, a great view. How on earth these stones were transported up here is a great mystery. Somehow, the Incas got it done. Now it's my turn.

"Remember The Night In Paris"
Paris, France – October 1999

I am having a difficult time finding my way back to the Paris restaurant, where I left Teresa almost an hour ago. We'd gone out to eat, our first night here, and had a terrible meal – very rare meat! When it was time to pay – I realized that I'd left my money at the hotel. Finally, I'm back and taking care of the tab. It is a lot easier returning to the hotel, which is only half mile from the Seine River. We trek up three flights of stairs and soon to bed.

It is morning. With camera and tripod, I'm walking down to the Seine River. The sun is coming up, as I photograph the Pontinuff Bridge with the Palace of Justice behind it. The street lamps across the bridge are picturesque. Breakfast with Teresa, and then a subway ride to Sacre Coeur, a Roman Catholic Cathedral, high above the city. From here we are heading to the Cimetiere du Pere La Chaise, where the grave of rock 'n roll legend, Jim Morrison of the Doors is. At his simple tombstone, there's a young man, probably in his early twenties with a jam box listening to "L.A. Woman", and a crowd of about thirty fans and tourists waiting to pay their respects. From here, we are taking the metro and are getting off close to the Eiffel Tower. Within minutes we are standing under it. As the sun begins to set, we head back to the Seine, finding the Pont Alexandre III Bridge for the perfect foreground. Minutes after sunset, the lamps have turned on. After a long day of walking, riding buses and the Metro, we are having a romantic moment, watching the Eiffel Tower in all its glory.

"Towering Over The Thames"
London, England ~ June 2000

Darkness has finally come to Great Britain. It is mid-summer, and the sun sets here, around 10:30 P.M. Standing by the Thames River, Leanne and I are watching as the lights of London Towne turn on, a photograph I was hoping to get. It's late, but we're going to ride the Big Ferris Wheel before retiring for the short night of sleep. I awaken at 5:30 A.M. and let Leanne sleep in, as I head back down to the river to check out the Tower Bridge. The sky is cloudy; there will be no sunrise this morning. I'm going back to the hotel to catch a few more hours of sleep, before having breakfast. The food here is terrible, the absolute worst of any trip to date. I've come down with some real serious stomach pain. Mid-day, we head back down to the river. As we walk along, a man taps me on the shoulder and points to the water below- a dead body is floating past us. Within minutes, a helicopter is arriving and they are pulling the body from the river. We move on. A quick visit to Buckingham Place, amazed at the guards, who won't even blink. Now hoping beyond hope that something happens to break up this overcast sky. Sunset is about an hour from now. We grab a quick dinner and go down to the good viewing point of the Tower Bridge. There are now dark storm clouds about. I look to the west and see a tad bit of clearing. The sun peaks through for a moment, throwing light on the bridge. Behind it, an ominous sky. What a grand finale.

"When Dreams Take Shape"
Prague, Czech Republic - October 2000

I'm leaving the Charles Bridge for the third morning in a row, a bit discouraged. It has rained here the first two, and this morning the sun came up without a cloud in the sky. The shot I want requires me to shoot into the sunrise, but today is too bright. I have just one day left to come up with the mission of this trip: a great shot of the bridge. If it takes all four mornings here, so be it. I've come on this trip alone for the first time. My hotel is a good mile and a half walk from the river on the Old Town side. I've just crossed over into the Little Quarter. Egg sandwich for breakfast and then back to work. I keep thinking about my desire to hop aboard a train here and head to Slavakia for the day. Eight hours of travel and four on the ground? I'll stick to the Prague Castle, not far from where I am. But first, I must take a few shots of the John Lennon Mural, with tons of signatures all over the wall. A small, but a meaningful tribute to one of the greats. Up the long hill passing many souvenir shops. Finally, I arrive at the castle. There are so many tourists here. I'm taking a few shots here, a few there. Finished, I head back down the hill toward the Charles Bridge. It's packed with more people. The vendors are out selling small paintings of the bridge that they drew, for $10-$20.

Back in Old Town, I am spending the evening, having a really good meal for $8 American dollars, way better than the Big Mac I had for $16 last year in Switzerland! Now it's time to shop. The marionettes they sell here are wonderful. I'll add some garnet jewelry to that, and finally, a Franz Kafka book, "Contemplations" that I will read tonight.

It's about 6: 30 A.M. on October 22, 2000. I have awakened for my final day in the Czech Republic. Looking out the window, I'm seeing what looks like a carbon copy a yesterday. Little do I realize, but the outside air temperature is about 10 degrees colder than yesterday. I begin the trek, running tight on the 7:30 A.M. sunrise. As I turn the corner, down by the river, the bridge is only partly visible. A great layer

of fog is hovering above. My heart is beating fast with excitement. There are glorious old statues of Jesus and the saints that grace the sides. I make my way just past St. Joseph. This is my foreground, so I set up the camera, as the sun is rising through the fog. Oh no, fifty feet behind me is a large group of Japanese tourists getting ready to disperse. The vendors will be on the bridge very soon. The time has come for me to take the shot! Awesome. I can't wait to see the film.

"Where There Was Peace"
Mt. Evans, Colorado - September 2001

Time to open the booth. It's the second Sunday of September and I'm at the 2001 Castle Rock Arts Festival. It actually snowed here Friday night, and yesterday it rained on and off all day, not exactly the right conditions for an outdoor show. Damp and cold, sales were few.

But today it's been busy. Business is cooking. Couldn't be happier. Big Bronco game today and I've got to get home to watch the highlights, feeling great about the day. Turning on the TV this evening, I'm learning the news is bad, at least here in the Denver sports world. Star receiver, Ed McCaffrey has been injured and expected out for the season. Many in Denver are expressing the misery they are feeling about this. Contemplating the rest of the Bronco season, I head to bed. Tomorrow I'm going to drive 60 miles up to Summit Lake at Mt. Evans to catch a sunrise. Up at 5 A.M., I'm off. First to Idaho Springs, then Echo Lake. The drive from there is getting hairy, a testy road with no guardrails and steep drop offs. I'm happy to arrive safely at Summit Lake.

This place should light up shortly as the minutes pass. It sits just below the peak of Mt. Evans, the most visible fourteener seen from Denver, Colorado. It's now about 8:30 A.M. and the sun has begun to twinkle in the meadow, the lake giving a sense of peace.

After note: I've shot my film, and get back in the car at about 8:50 A.M. As I begin to head back down, the radio has a lot of static. I manage to make out some words about a plane crash, then something about the World Trade Towers.

"Lost At Sea"
Kangaroo, Island, Australia - August 2002

Last night, Chris and I witnessed a spectacular sunset at one of Australia's national treasures, the Twelve Apostles. Today, we are hugging the southern coast as tight as we can, heading for Adelaide, where we'll take a ferry to Kangaroo Island. As the sun begins to set, we are gliding across the water. Known for its high population of kangaroos, the island's beauty is remarkable. Now that we're here, we now have to drive an hour, through darkness, to reach our hotel in the little town of Kingscote. The air feels so fresh here. After a good night's sleep we awaken early to begin our three hour trip to Finder's Chase National Park on the eastern end of the island. Within a few miles of town, we pass a junkyard hosting lots of wrecked cars. We are told that many car rental companies do not do business here due to the many accidents with wildlife. Along the way three kangaroos and three wallabies, all at different times, hop across the road in front of us, nearly causing my heart to jump out of my body. We have decided to stop at Seal Bay, where a good hundred sea lions are basking in the sun on the beach. After spending about an hour and a half here, we continue toward our destination. Once arriving, I am simply mystified by the sound of the sea waves crashing against the coastline. Here, there is a lighthouse. Chris spots a whale in the ocean, as we descend the many steps to the bottom of the rocks. After a little exploring, we find an arch looking out to sea, and there, playing in the water, are a number of New Zealand fur seals. I tell Chris " I am lost at sea, when I die, scatter my ashes here".

"When You Wish"
Barcelona, Spain - September 2002

It is a hot day for late summer. Frustrated, Teresa and I are at the airline office in downtown Barcelona, trying to find out what has happened to two of our bags, lost on our flight from Granada. One contains my tripod, essential in shooting a 645 camera. We wait and wait, still no word on our bags. Finally, we leave and decide to climb the 300 plus stairs of the Basilica de La Sagrada Familia church, one of Gaudi's masterpieces, here in the city. Three shinny big bizarre looking towers have winding stairs that lead us up. Probably, 300 steps or more. Supposedly they connect here at some point. After a bit, we've had our share of Gaudiness for the day. Checking back at the hotel, still no bags. Dinner, a walk, and then bedtime.

Morning has come, with the same old news- no bags! I'm feeling very burned out on all the Gaudi weird architecture around. We decide to take a train down to "Las Ramblas", the big street festival that goes 24/7. I take only my Canon 35mm with me. This, I can hand hold. We arrive around noon. Walking along, we are enjoying the mimes that entertain us with their stillness. Soon I am aware of this magical couple drawing a crowd. The woman is all dressed in blue, as is her hair. "And the blue Bubble Lady blows her bubbles into the sky, always searching for wishes that haven't come true."

"In Light Of The Unexpected"
Stockholm, Sweden - September, 2003

The pouring rain has awakened me just before 1:00 A.M. We have been here in Hamnoy, a small village in Norway's Lofoten Islands, for four days and the precipitation began about 10:30 A.M. on day one. Two hours of magical blue light the first day we where here and it hasn't stopped raining since. I better try to get back to sleep. We have to fly from the airport here to Oslo in the morning and then an afternoon flight to Stockholm for two nights, before returning to the States. Teresa wakes before me and has the coffee brewing for our journey to yet another country. Though the weather here is drizzly, clearing is the forecast for our early evening landing.

Teresa has developed a headache on the plane, and is not feeling well. Upon landing in Sweden, the rain continues, and my mood turns sour very quickly. Arriving at our hotel on the bay, Teresa suggests that, despite the way she feels, we should go out on the town, and forget about the shoot for now. After all, it is night time. Sounds like a good idea. We've had what we thought was an enjoyable dinner, but then T's headache seems to be getting worse. We must find a pharmacy for her. Walking for hours in the drizzling rain in Gamla Stan (Old Stockholm) we finally find a pharmacy that is open until 11:00 P.M. Glad we brought an umbrella. Now we must find our way back to our hotel. We can cut through the Stockholm Castle to save some time. It's just before midnight as we arrive at the old fortress. We're anxious to get back and to get T to bed. As we cross the cobblestone sidewalks, I stop to look at something that has caught my eye. It's an alley way, lit by an old lantern. There's a puddle that's reflecting the light, as raindrops trickle down upon it. I have to come back here and shoot this. T says, "You're crazy, it's midnight". I escort her back to the hotel, grab my camera equipment and return to the scene, 45 minutes later. The rain has stopped, at last! It is now a near perfect reflection in the water. This could be the shot of the trip.

"End Of Darkness"
Angkor Wat, Cambodia - February 2004

After spending a short night in Bangkok, we are now coming in for a landing at the little airport in Siem Reep, Cambodia. With me is John Steineger, the husband of my hair stylist, who stepped in at the last minute to take this trip. A guide is meeting us here at the airport. Booten is his name, and his favorite word is "Yuppers". He says it pretty frequently, even in the middle of a sentence. We've checked into the hotel, caught a quick nap and have paid the $40 fee to get into the Temple. Miles and miles of ruins, over a thousand years old, cover the landscape. 2:30 P.M. and the sky is quite hazy, yet bright. 45 minutes later I decide to give it a try and break out the camera. As I'm photographing a long gallery, a man approaches and starts talking with Booten. Within minutes Booten informs me that I can't use the big camera without written permission from the local government. We decide we better go with them. A woman and a young man are in the police station, bombarding me with questions like "why the big camera?" I actually find myself having to lie here "I shoot occasionally for magazines and travel agents." The policeman now wants to see the camera. John, who is waiting for me in another room, brings it to the table. I am trying to convince them that the camera is not big, just bigger than a 35mm. The conversation is going nowhere. I need to fill out this form and ask the "director" for permission. We are about done here. Booten says he'll check back in an hour to hear the answer. Heading back to the Temple of Ankor Wat for the final hour of daylight, we come upon a precious woman sitting by the entrance. She has no hands and no feet. How humble. Booten says, "She walks here, ½ mile, yuppers, every day, to sit here." It has been so hot today that my cloths are drenched with sweat. The government doesn't have an answer yet.

Back to the motel to our $35 a night dive, a decent dinner and bed. We are meeting Booten at 5:30 A.M. to head back to the temple. I can now see the silhouettes of five towers, reflecting in a pond. Nearby is a much smaller structure, and as I step inside, there is a strong ray of light shooting across the floor. We're going to take the gamble here. Out with the big camera, the Pentax 645, without that written permission.

"Pure Island Ecstasy"
Big Island of Hawaii - February 2005

Teresa and I have come to the Big Island of Hawaii as a recovery trip from an on foot accident I had with an out-of-control motorcycle. Call it rehab, but of course, I've taken my camera, feeling very passionate about getting a lava shot. Two days ago, I tried a helicopter ride. Scary, since the door of the copter remained open as we flew over the Pu'u O'o Crater. My injured right leg was nearly hanging out. The pilot told us not to let a camera lens outside because Madame Pele has been known to steal such things.

After this experience, I was convinced that we had to walk out on the lava field, about 2 miles. Since I was still on crutches, Teresa and I decided we would need help. We called our son Chris, who was living in California at the time and asked him if he'd like to join us in Hawaii. I had sufficient air miles to book him an immediate flight.

Today is the final day of this adventure. Chris has been here since yesterday. A morning coffee at Borders and a sandwich at the deli, we are on our way down Chain of Craters Road to the coastline. It's about 4 P.M., Chris has dropped T and I off, while he parks the car. We lucked out by getting one of the park rangers to drive us down the half mile of road before the lava starts. We pass many who are walking. I choose to try this with my cane, instead of the crutches. Chris is carrying the camera gear in the lead. After more than an hour of navigating over the lava, we can see steam rising from the ocean. Suddenly, a flare of red. It's getting dark and we can see the lava, bright red, not too far from us. Breaking out the camera, I shoot about 5 rolls of film, until it is dark. So thankful to Chris for his help, we make our way back to the ranger station, happy to have accomplished what we did.

Now that it's the next morning, before our flight home, we are driving back to Kapahoe Bay, a spot we had visited twice before, but hadn't yet had the desired light. This morning will be different. We carefully walk out across some lava to get next to the water. Beauty at its best. The waves are breaking into this tropical shoreline. Pure island ecstasy.

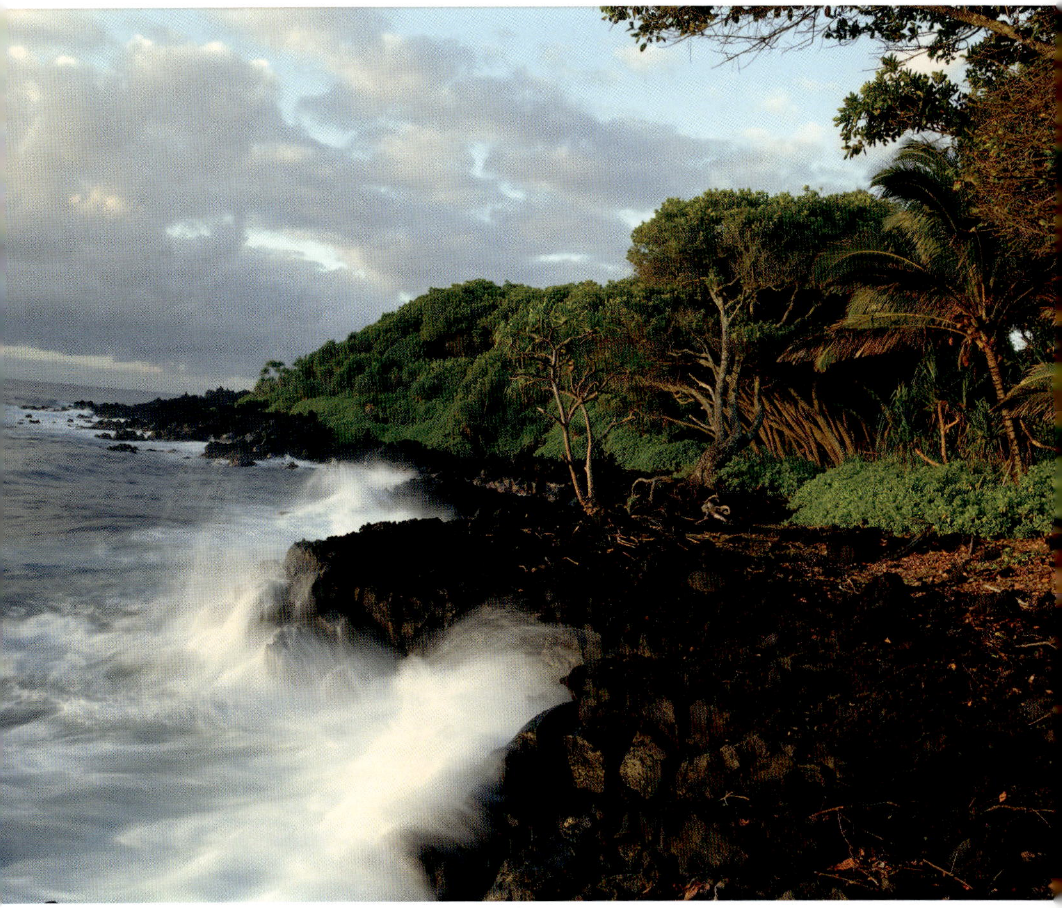

"Journey Of A Lifetime"
The Great Wall of China at Mutianyu
September 2005

We have just landed in China, Beijing International Airport. My Cambodian partner, John Steineger, is with me again. One big reason I took this journey is because a Craig Hospital doctor, Jim Berry, put a challenge to me: "Pick a place in the world you've always wanted to photograph, go there and do it within a year of your accident." For me, the answer was easy "The Great Wall of China". Now we are here for the challenge, September 21st, 2005, just short of a year. I'll still need the help of a cane and John, carrying the gear, to make it up the many steps. How many? Getting that information was nearly impossible. There were two basic choices on where to go, Badaling or Mutianyu, the latter, with more hills and less tourists. That was our decision. Now that we're checked into the hotel, we'll cruise around town, mostly on foot. Last on today's agenda is a visit to The Forgotten City. It is extremely crowded, on a dismal kind of day and the air quality is worse than bad. A good excuse to keep the stop short. Back to the hotel, we are a bit wet from some rain. Dinnertime and our first chance to try real Chinese food. We are quite happy with the meal. Time to crash; it will be a short night.

We're awakened at 3 A.M. by an alarm clock. Shutting it off with a hard swat, the next sounds I hear is that of pouring rain. We both, though barely awake, look at each other with the same thought of going back to bed. However, that was twenty five minutes ago and now we're in the lobby waiting for our ride. An hour and a half of driving, well outside the Beijing city limits, has put us at the trailhead at Mutianyu. There's a cable car here that opens at 8 A.M., long after sunrise, if there is one. The rain has actually slowed down to a drizzle. We find the first steps that lead up, as they quickly disappear into an eerie mist. At the top is the Great Wall of China. The steps are big for little people. John must see a look in my face because he speaks "C'mon Andy, we've come all this way". With my cane in hand, I begin the climb, ascending 792 difficult steps to the top. It is so foggy, we can barely see a few feet in front of us. I've been told that once one arrives at the top, the wall begins to crawl across the mountains. It is now 6 A.M., the sun should be trying to breakthrough within minutes. It's getting lighter as we speak. The fog is pulling back. With total wonder John and I both look, as the ball of the just risen sun, is seen through the mist in the east. The wall winds down the mountainside and up another. Sunshine now on the wall, graced with shadows. Thank you, Lord. This is a heavenly moment. We made it.

"A Pilgrim's Message"
Vishan Ghat India - April 2006

It has been a long and difficult trip to India. The poverty and the filth have been a lot to handle. We see many beggars, who have nothing. For now, we are settling down by the river that runs aside the Taj Mahal. It is nearly sunset. For my daughter Leanne, and I, this is our last night of the trip. Tomorrow, we will head back to New Delhi. We have befriended a young man named Bal Kishan and his younger brother, Brijesh. As the sun sets, it is hazy and less than stunning. We say goodnight to our company and return back to the hotel in Agra.

As morning arrives, we head back to the river for one more look at the Taj and say farewell to our friends. It is about a 6 to 8 hour ride to the big city and I ask our driver if he would stop at a lakeside village called Vishan Ghat, where pilgrims come. We arrive at our destination, the driver parks the car and informs us that we need to take a tut-tut to the lake. Doing as instructed, we are having a very shaky ride down narrow streets. The tut-tut begins to make funny noises, and then comes to a stop. The driver leaves us alone to get some help. We are waiting as tons of people surround us. Holding the camera gear close to me, I feel the sense of fear. At last, a scary looking guy with a painted face approaches us and says "Come, I am to take you to Vishan Ghat". Arriving, we now see a temple, surrounded by brightly colored buildings with unique arches. The villagers, dressed in wild custom outfits, greet us. They are surrounding us and want Leanne to go into the lake water for some tribal ceremony. A strange moment, for sure. We talk our way out of this, and things are working out fine. Relieved we begin to walk around the area and I see a turquoise green and pink arch with inscriptions written all over. I don't have a clue how this is all interpreted. It could be an ancient Indian Language. Out with the camera, and away goes the shutter, glad for now to be safe and unharmed.

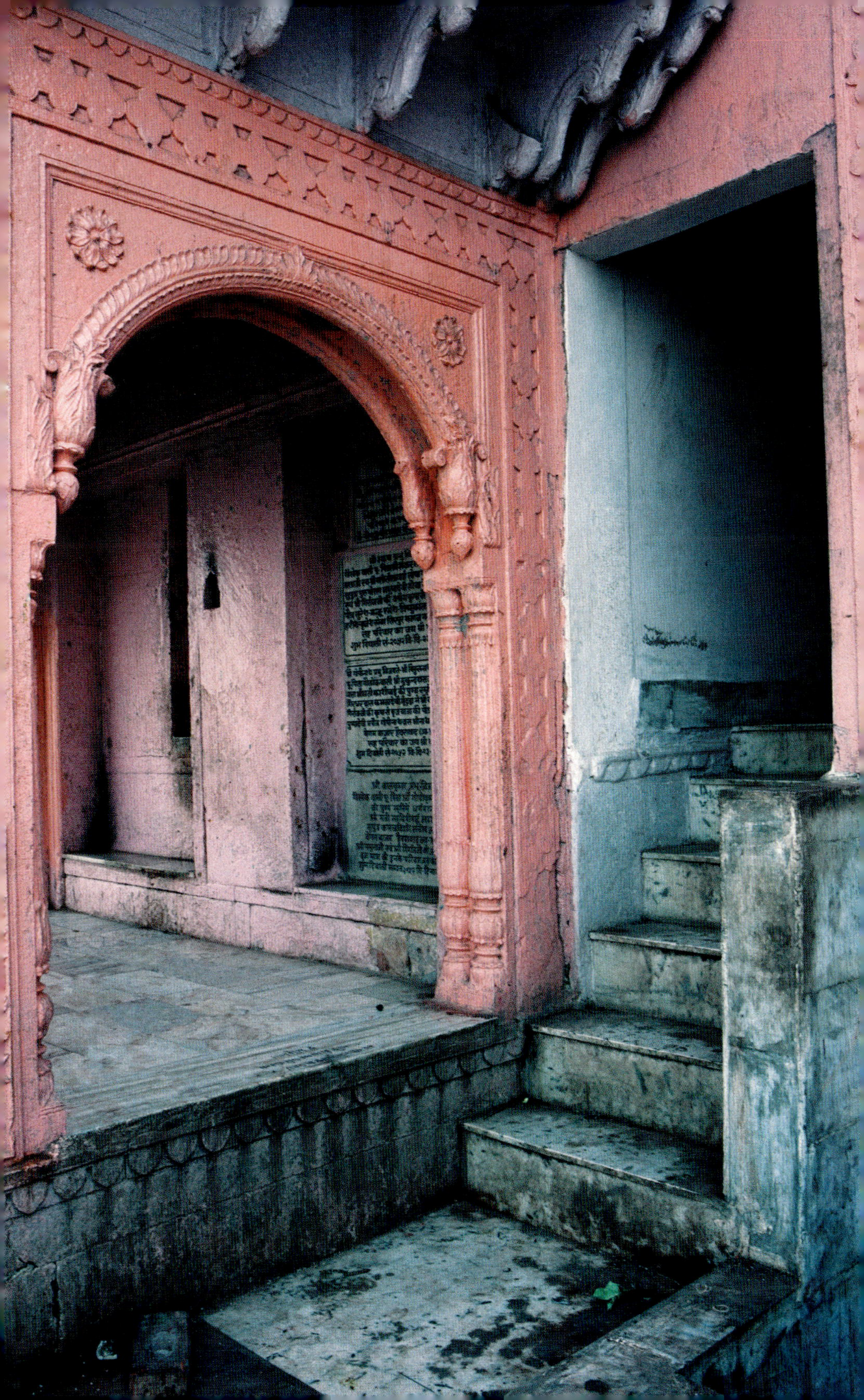

"Vow Of Silence"
Muckross Abbey, Ireland - October 2006

We have now been in Ireland for 4 nights, two at the Cliffs of Mohrer (only place overseas that I've returned to). I took what I hope to be a great shot of this wonder. This time, Teresa and our 9-year-old daughter, Nikki, are with me. We're on the western end of the Ring of Kerry, planning for a boat ride tomorrow to Skellig Michael, a couple of small islands off the coast. It has the ruins of an old monastery, which is reached by hiking 600 steps up the side of a small mountain. Arriving from Kilarney, we are now in Knightstown. I take a picture of an old clock tower, quite red in color. A decision is made to head to the coast and catch a sunset with Skellig Michael silhouetted. We book a room, and a boat, for tomorrow's adventure. The weather report is for rain and wind. Morning comes around, we find our captain who is giving us the bad news. "I have enough problems with people getting sea sick on a calm day, hell if I'm going out today". We're all heavily disappointed; this was to be the highlight of the trip. Time to pack our bags and head back to Kilarney. Stopping at Kilarney National Park, the goal here is to go back into the woods and take some shots of the old Muckross Abbey. What an incredible forest there is here in the park. Two horses and an old wagon take us to the abbey. This ride reminds me of Gandalf riding through the Shire. We arrive at the abbey in about 15 minutes. The driver lets us out. There is a graveyard here from years ago. Nikki has some chills. Going inside the abbey, there are four paths making a square around a bizarre looking tree. A fence keeps visitors from touching it. Looking down the corridor, I too am getting a weird feeling here, but I'm ready to take a shot of the white and gray arches.

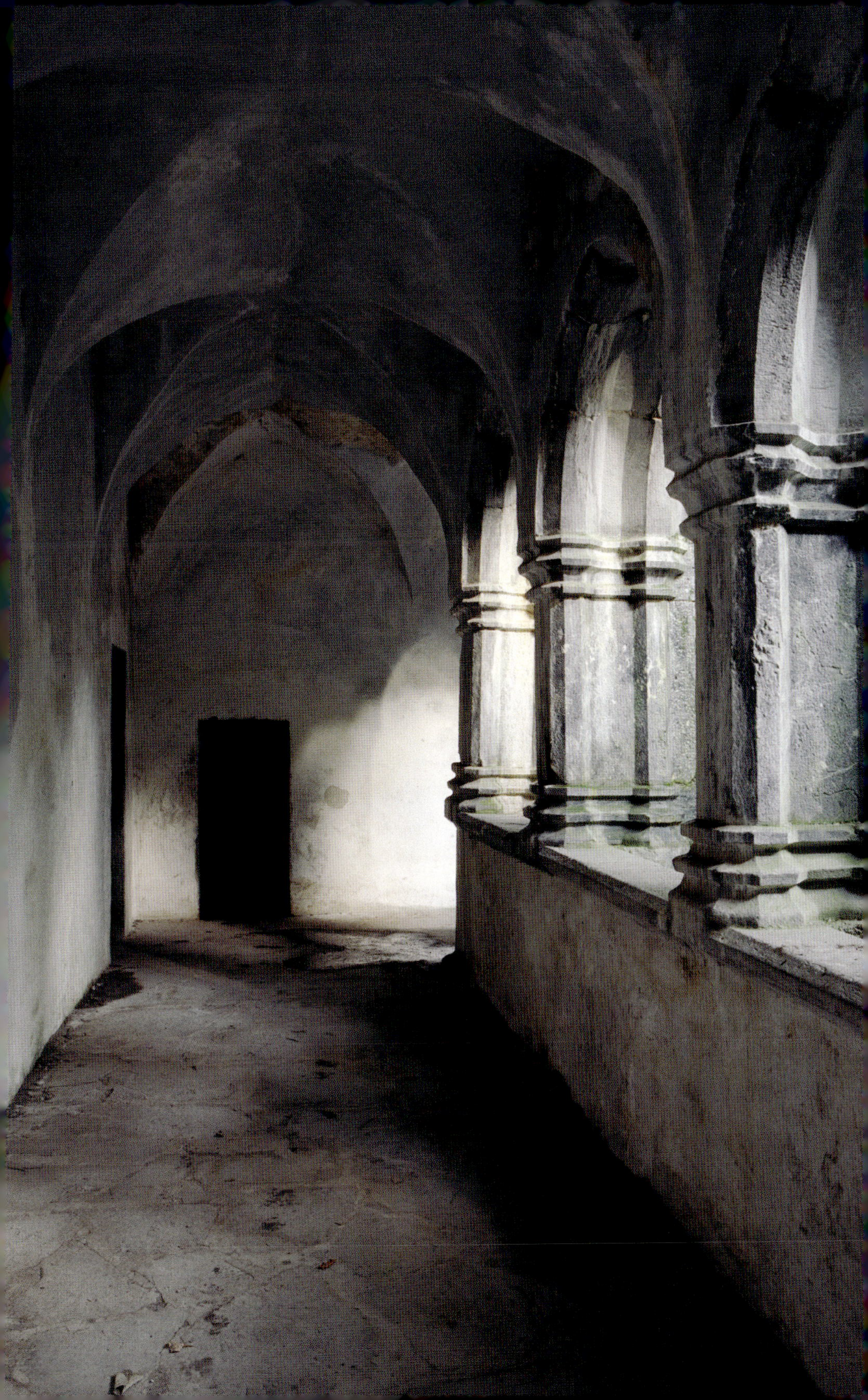

"In Search Of The Absolute Dawn"
Torres del Paine, Chile - March 2007

This time around, John Steineger and I met in Santiago. I had just flown in from the states and he had come down a week early to do some exploring of his own. Together we flew to the southern tip of Chile and stayed a night in Puentas Arenas. Originally, we had planned to stay here two nights, but we've found the town to be kind of seedy, so we'll be heading north to Puerto Natales today, where we'll spend the night. Before we leave this area, we're taking a drive along the Straights of Magellan, where we stop and photograph a couple of shipwrecks along the coast. Heading north the flat landscape has changed to mountains to the east and west of us.

After a five hour drive, and a cloudy sunset, we check into our hotel, have dinner and crash, ready for an early morning. Awakening at 4 A.M., we have about three hours to drive east and reach the park by sunrise. A fairly straight road has turned awfully curvy, and a clear sky has turned increasingly cloudy as we reach the park boundaries. As we find the mountains I had wished to photograph, a lot of fog has settled in, and the Towers, as they're called, are not visible. Only Mt. Almirate Nieto can be seen. We wait for perhaps an hour, and then begin to pack away the camera gear, when a sudden red glow appears at the base. Quickly resetting up the camera and tripod, I run through the five remaining shots in my roll of 15. By the time I can change the film, the glow of red is gone. "Remember this one" I say to John.

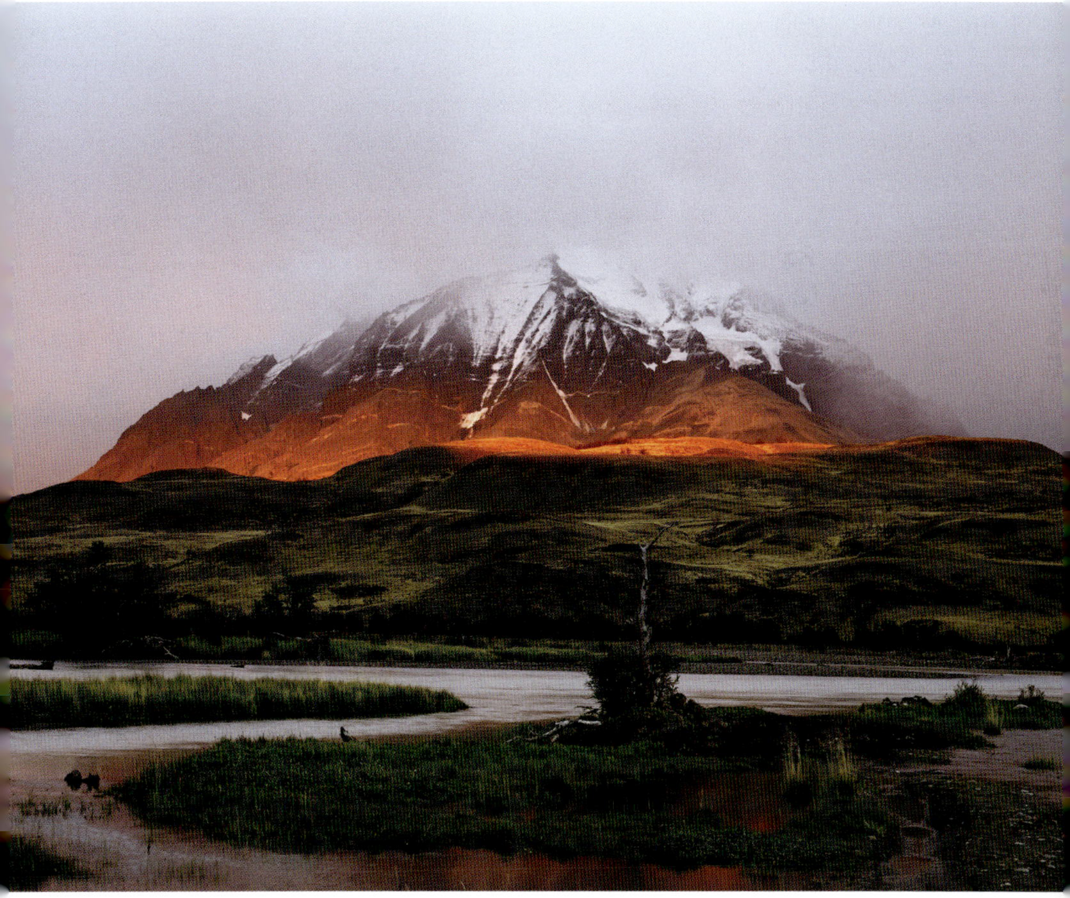

"Let The Night Begin"
Bar Harbor, Maine – October 2007

We've just finished dinner at a restaurant in the charming coastal town of Bar Harbor, Maine. All kinds of cool boats can be seen docked in the harbor. Food here is great. Tomorrow I'll have my new camera, however we have to drive to a Fed Ex station in Bangor to pick it up. Saturday morning, after being here for two rainy days with Teresa and 10-year-old Nikki, we drove up to Cadillac Mountain to visit the first place the sun can be seen rising in the U.S. I wasn't ready for the extreme gusts of wind that come across the mountain top and down went the tripod and camera. The back of the camera had been destroyed. After extensive phone calls, I found an outfit in Atlanta that could send me a new body for a mere $750. An expensive misfortune. I ordered it, and now we've been here at Acadia National Park, just scouting around.

Awakening to the fresh morning air here in Maine, we are planning our day. We have been invited to a couple's home, who I met at the Rio Grande Arts Festival in Albuquerque last week. They have blueberry fields on their property; this is a big thing here. After a couple hours visiting, we are driving to Bangor to pick up our expected package, listening to John Fogerty's new CD. The camera is here on time. We're heading back to Acadia to photograph the Bar Harbor Head Lighthouse at sunset. Arriving, I see a dark cloudbank in the western sky. This is good. We have parked our rental car, and are heading down some big rocks to the water's edge, just below the lighthouse. Setting up the camera, I fire away as the sun disappears below the horizon. Nice, but bright. We pack the gear and climb part of the way up with our backs to the west. An old man sitting on a rock, raises his arm and points to the sky behind us. The sky has illuminated with color. The red signal light of the lighthouse has just come on. Let the night begin.

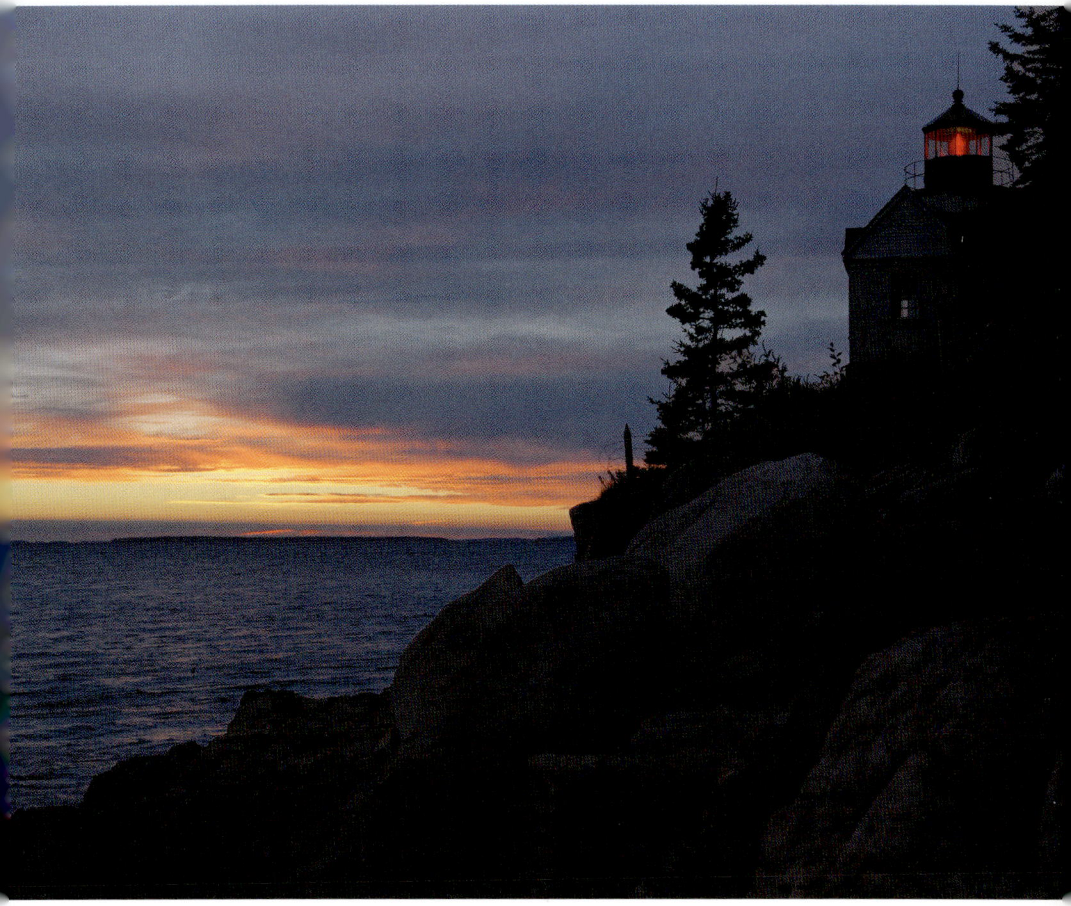

"The Book Well Read"
Jerusalem, Israel - March 2008

After spending the night in Amon, Jordan, Chris and I are being driven to the Israeli border. Our plans are to spend 24 hours there, then return to Jordan and head to Petra. A lot of forms to fill out here before passing over the bridge. After crossing, we are having an issue with Israeli security. The guide who is supposed to meet us here is nowhere to be found. It's my big bag with the tripod in it that has them freaked out. They're not sure just what is in it. So, after a 45-minute delay, we are good to go. Finally the guide hooks up with us and asks whether we want to see the Church of the Nativity in Bethlehem. My answer is "sure". After about a thirty-minute drive from the airport, we come to a guard gate. There is this humongous machine gun with lots of rounds pointed right at us! "What's this?" I ask. Our guide responds, "It is Palestine". It totally escaped me that Bethlehem became part of Palestine in 1993. We are stopping at a gift shop before going to the church. Here I'm spending about $500 on crosses for the family and myself. Fast talking salesman here in the shop, but how can you not? Now, on to the church. I'm here in the big room. I say to Chris "I can't believe I'm standing here and photographing in Bethlehem in the spot where Jesus was born". Back to Jerusalem, and a visit to the Garden of Gesetheme and the Grotto of the Betrayal. Now to the Seven Arches hotel on the Mt. of Olives. I am hoping to get a skyline shot from here, but there are clouds and more important, lots and lots of cranes. It's becoming time to eat and sleep tonight.

With sunrise, I shoot the Dome of the Rock from the hotel grounds. Breakfast and our guide arrives. Before seeing the Stations of the Cross, we want to visit the Wailing Wall. Our guide tells us to go by ourselves up to the Wall. He says, "I am Palestinian, and I will not go there." We proceed alone. There are many Rabbis here; one I notice is in real deep prayer. He is holding the Bible up against the Wall.

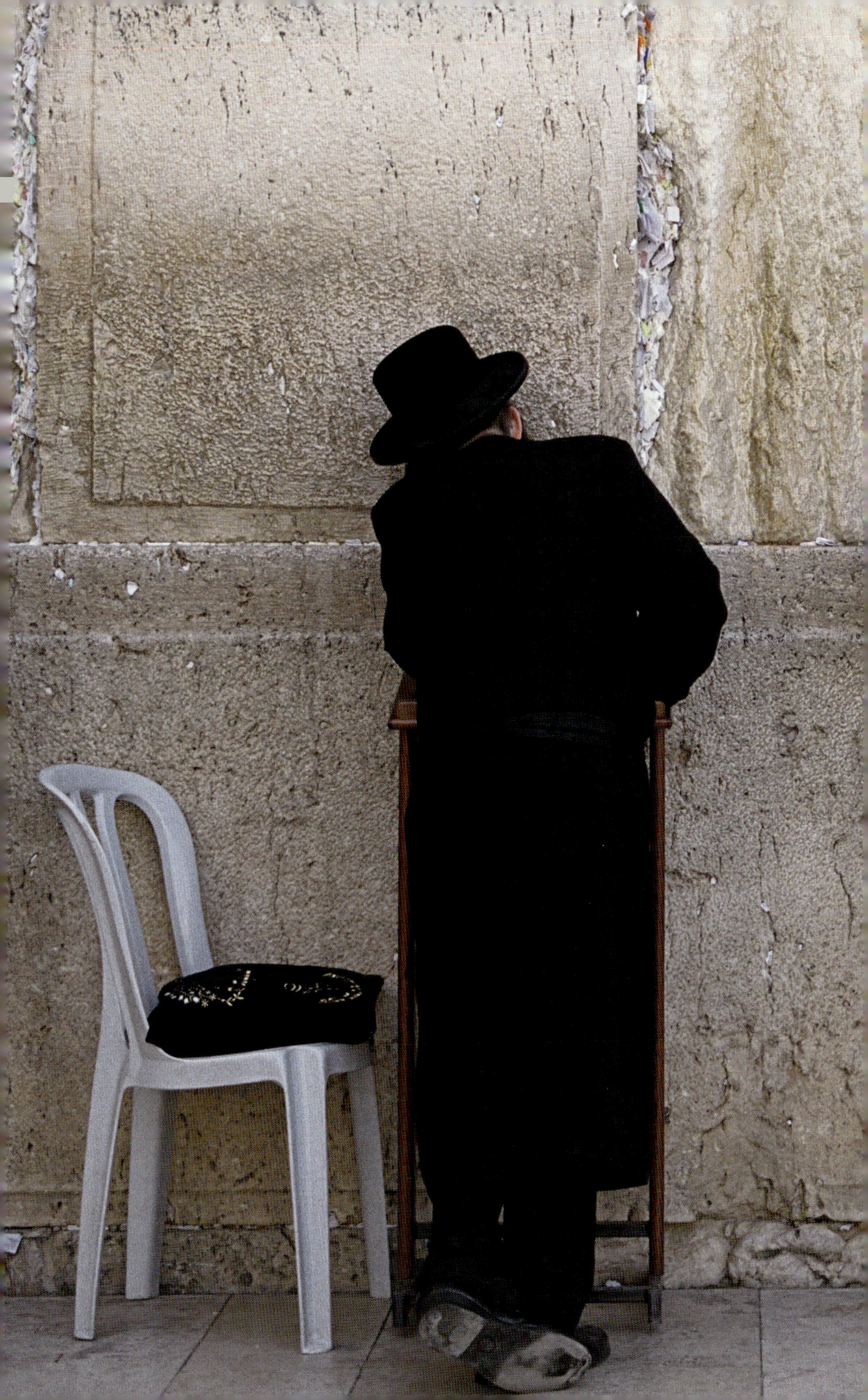

"Back In B.C."
Petra, Jordan - April 2008

Chris and I have just returned from a 3 mile round trip hike to see one of the Seven Wonders of the World, the Treasury at Petra. A beautiful trail winds down through a canyon, known as the SIQ, where I photographed a couple of hours ago. We are now meeting with our travel agent, Ramzi of Jordan Tours. They have carefully planned out this trip for me, based on what I wanted to shoot, including the Israel part of it. We are being introduced to the man who will guide us on tomorrow's journey to a high place. His name is Muhammed, and was one of the extra kids used in the movie, "Indiana Jones and the Temple of Doom." He tells us that "Indiana Jones and the Last Crusade" was filmed at Petra. Now he's a location manager for most movies filmed in Jordan. So as sunset approaches, he takes us up above the city for a breathtaking view. Once darkness comes, we are having dinner at the Petra Place Restaurant, a truly wonderful meal, where we helped prepare the food. The soup is some of the best I've tasted, anywhere. One of the guides is talking about entertaining Senator John McCain, President Bill Clinton and Hillary, recently.

It's the following morning and we've met Muhammed at the Visitor Center. We start the climb going down the same path that winds down to the SIQ. Shortly we break away on a path to the left. The trail is getting pretty rocky. 3 ½ years after having been run into by a motorcycle, I'm needing some assistance getting up and over some of the boulders that are now the way to go. With help from Muhammed and Chris, I'm making it up to our viewpoint. Down below the cliff, is a far different view of the Treasury. We are literally standing on the edge, where we set up the tripod. Scary. There are people at the base of these amazing ruins. Muhammed whistles. They disappear into the shadows except for the two guards. Muhammed explains to us that sunlight is only on the face of the Treasury for less than an hour between 9 A.M. and 10 A.M., as the light slips away from the top. Muhammed holds me by the belt as I take two rolls of treasured film.

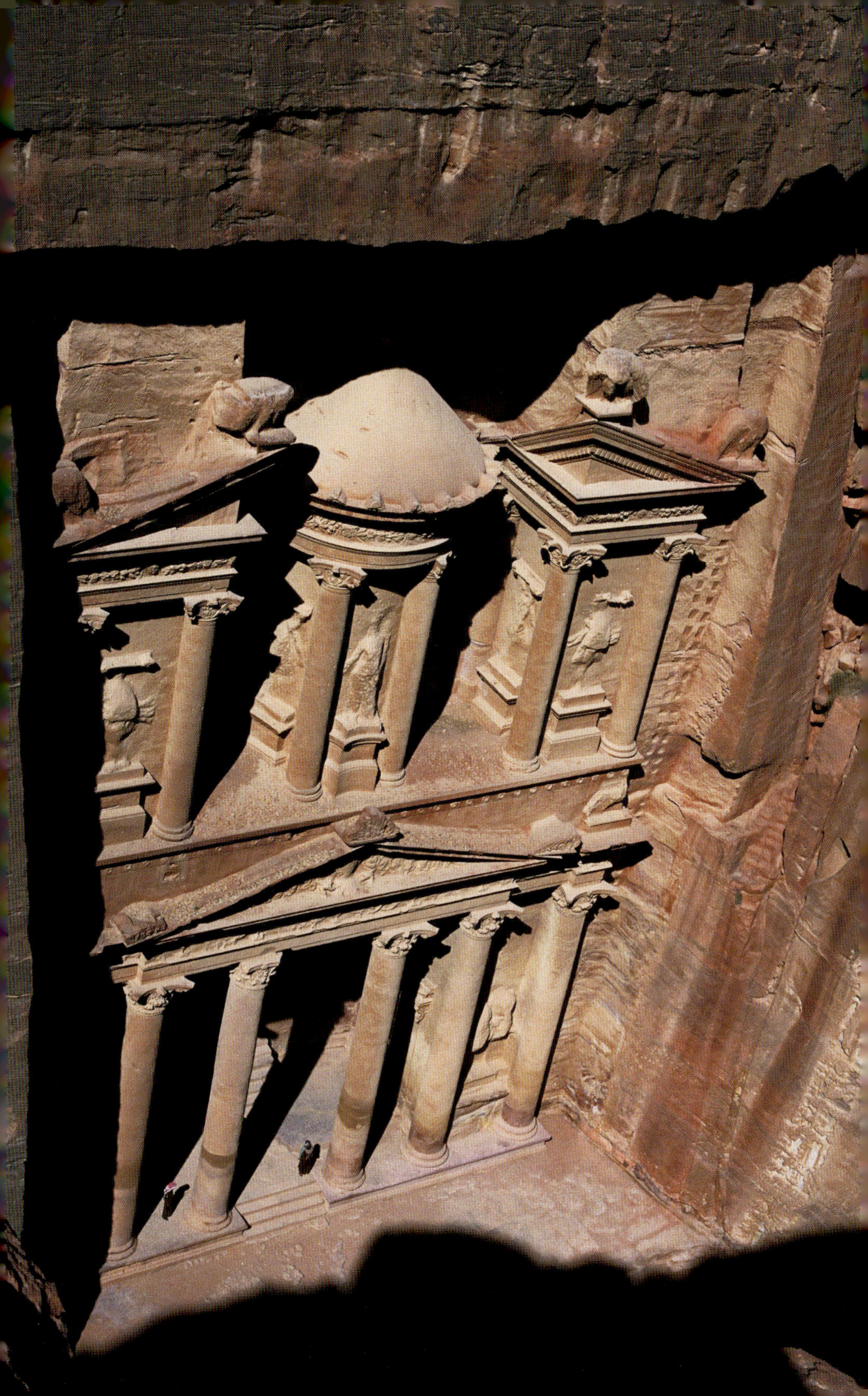

Acknowledgements

Editor: Lu Soto Mahan

Cover photo: Patty Penta

Design: Jennifer Heagle with Alternative Press

    I would like to especially thank my family for being so supportive over the years. Teresa, Chris, Leanne and Nikki have all traveled with me on these shoots. My close friends John Steineger, Mark Kramer, Gilbert Doctoroff and Mark Nichols have also been important parts of the travels. Thanks to Leo and Michelle Wurschmidt for their continued, wonderful work on our web-site. And to H.A. Thompson, thank you for your years of friendship, inspiration, and always your strong, sensible advice. All of this could not have been possible without a good Lab. Mike Roberts of Fine Print and the Reed family - thank you!

    This book is dedicated to the doctors and staff at Craig and Swedish hospitals for twice saving my life.

Andy Marquez

About the Author and Photographer

A Brooklyn hospital is where I was born on August 24th, 1951. Five days later, I became the son of Philip and Gloria Marquez, who lived in a two bedroom simple house in Bayside, New York. We were near Alley Pond Park, a city owned wooded area a mile deep and three long, right on the outskirts of Queens. I grew up an only child, since my parents never chose to adopt again. Dad was a Roman Catholic and Mom, a Brooklyn Jew. He worked as a production manager for Harper and Rowe book publishers in the city. Mom was a housewife for the time. I started in public school, P.S. 213, right up the street. My day was school, then home to hang out in the woods, building tree forts and finding new paths with friends, Adam and Seth. We'd play whiffle and softball in the street, as we loved our hometown Yankees, Mickey and Roger, hitting all those homeruns. Mom converted to Catholicism and I transferred to St. Robert Bellarmine School in the fourth grade, mostly to be taught by nuns. We had to wear uniforms, white shirts and ties. The elementary school years passed with little drama. I was one of only 13 boys who were accepted at Bishop Reilly High School, where I joined the Film Society. I began to use an 8mm movie camera loaned to me by my Uncle "Onion", Mom's younger brother. Norman was in the movie business; even did some work on "Midnight Cowboy". He always told me how important the light was. I made a few shorts with neighborhood friends, using the nature, just across the street, as the settings. Little did I know that the seeds of my future had been planted.

When I was 16, I became quite sick with encephalitis, followed by a diabetic coma. I remember watching the movie "The Birds" the night things took a bad turn. I'm sure to this very day that I saw the bright light. When I came out of it, I remember the first words I said to Mom " I guess I won't see Him today." I missed a few weeks of school, and began to write for their poetry magazine called "Moments". I won an award for my piece, "Off On A Tangent". "The Lord of the Rings" was introduced to me in an advanced English class, and I became a huge fan. When the time came to think about college, I decided I wanted to be a writer. Wishes do come true. Sometimes, it just takes a little time.

My folks and I vacationed to the 1,000 Islands, New York and to Florida's Sanibal Island, usually each, once a year, during high school. I thought it would be cool to go to a College that was located half way between New York and Florida. And so, I chose the University of South Carolina in good ol' Columbia. Dad bought me a 35 mm Minolta SRT 101 for my 18th birthday, the summer before leaving for college. I planned to use it on campus. Majoring in Journalism, one of my courses was black and white photography, which involved a lot of fun darkroom work.

And the music. I loved the late 60's and early seventies. There has never been a time of so much passion. There was a cause; at least in people's heads, this was some kind of revolution. I joined the school concert committee where in our first year, we changed the venue from the Tams and the Drifters to Chicago and Steppenwolf. We actually booked Chicago for $4,000, before their second album peaked and sold tickets through the fraternities for $1.50. I was asked to be the concert photographer for Mountain, when they came to town. Continuing forward, I photographed Gordon Lightfoot, Johnny Winter, Judy Collins, Grand Funk, CCR, Jethro Tull and more. Recently, I resurrected the color slides and black and white negs from deep in my crawl space at home. (On March 30th, 2012, they were released for sale.) Soon, I began to write words for music a friend wrote. This didn't really go anywhere except that throughout my college years, I managed to start my own agency, Southern Trail Talent, booking a lot of fraternity gigs for local bands and emerging talent. This, I continued after graduation, because of the lack of available jobs in my field.

In 1974, Dad and my Mom, glorious Gloria, sold their house in Bayside and moved south, close to me in Myrtle Beach, S.C. By 1976, the Bee Gees were hot and the disco craze took over. I was working part time, waiting tables at Steak and Ale, and soon became the disco DJ in the lounge. The demand for the kind of music I was handling diminished, and I had to close the agency.

Searching for a new direction in my life, I found other opportunities including starting Columbia's first crepe house. Nothing was lasting more than 6 months before going belly up. Deciding to get my body in shape (it could only help my diabetes), I joined European Health Spas. Before long, I was working for them selling memberships. In 1978, this great manager I worked for, Shaw Davis, decided to leave European and open a club in Charlotte. He offered me a job at the International Fitness Center. This meant leaving the town where I lived for 9 years. Charlotte was a bigger city, a bit more metropolitan. And so, I moved north, to be the men's club manager. Before long we were hiring the ladies staff. I still remember the day when I first met this pretty green eyed red head, now my beloved wife of 30 years, Teresa Hamilton.

In 1981, we were both offered jobs by a firm called Cosmopolitan Lady in Houston. That Christmas Eve, I asked Teresa to be my wife. Difficult months followed as we were split up to different branches scattered all over the city. That year, 1982, Teresa's Mom, Anne, sadly passed away. In the spring, May 15th, Teresa and I married on Hilton Head Island. One of my former emerging talents, Larry Rhodes, sang Dan Fogelberg's "Leader of the Band", at the wedding. We honeymooned in Ft. Walton Beach and New Orleans as we made our way back to Texas. Later that year, we lost my Dad, Big Phil. Mom decided to stay in their condo in North Myrtle Beach.

We returned to Houston, jobless, but not for long. I was hired by World Wide Health Studies, as a Men's Club Manager, and turned around a failing enterprise. Having Fri-Sun off, Teresa and I began to travel around Texas, and with this came out the dusty old camera. Padre Island, Galveston Beach and Big Bend National Park became some of my first scenic places to photograph. I musn't forget the beautiful bluebonnet fields. The results were promising. What made us begin to sell them? Well, I guess it was one of those "it was meant to be" moments. On May 5th, 1984, we did our first show at the Houston Flea Market and made our first $25, in the art show business.

In October of 1984, we took a week vacation and did our first official photo-shooting trip. We left Houston and headed northwest in our 1982 customized maroon Ford Van with big windows. Spent our first night in New Mexico, sleeping in the van, on the west side of I-25 South between Santa Fe and Albuquerque. The next morning we were able to catch the International Hot Air Balloon Festival. From here we headed west on I-40 for a night in the Painted Desert, then one at the Grand Canyon, followed by a night each at the Saguaro National Monument in Tucson, and on the way back, White Sands, and Carlsbad Caverns. After this trip, we realized that living in Houston wasn't going to work, if this was the career we wished to pursue. My cousins Susan and Ray from my Dad's side of the family were living in Littleton, Colorado and invited us up for our first anniversary. Mom even flew out from Myrtle Beach. We fell in love with Colorado despite having a 10" snow storm on the day we were flying back.

Soon Teresa became pregnant with our first child, Christopher Philip. He was born on March 20th, 1985. On May 15th, on our 3rd Anniversary, we crossed over Raton Pass into Colorado, hauling a super packed van with a trailer. In the front, between us, was Chris, in his car seat and our Lhasa Apso, Pippin. We landed at Wolhurst Landing in Littleton. I had actually lined up a job with Bally's Health Club in Englewood prior to moving. What a high-pressure mess. The Denver area director would call me late at night and quiz me about my day's gross sales, and tomorrow's appointments.

The Evergreen Summerfest was one of the first shows we did in Colorado. So excited that we made $285, I quit my job at Bally's the following Monday and decided to go full time selling my photos.

A wood stove in the central room heated our rental condo. The first winter there, I remember icicles on our bedroom window. I also remember having so little money that we went down Santa Fe Drive a mile or so to buy $3 worth of wood at Silver Crown. This happened often. Labor Day weekend we had our first $1,000 show at the Taste of Colorado, which to this very day, has been an annual event.

Since Teresa's family lived outside of Charlotte in a little town called Marshville, and Mom was living at the beach, we decided to do some shows in Charlotte, driving 1600 miles cross country to a 3 day art fest called "Spring fest". The show was cancelled after a couple of years. One of Charlotte's finest voices, both on the air and in public, H.A. Thompson, had been a mentor and big collector, since we met about the time Teresa and I did. His advice paid off. We started making bi-annual trips to the Southern Spring and Christmas show. Over the years, I blew two transmissions on the road, one in Illinois and one, where I was first at the traffic light, exit 12 on I-70 in Kansas City rush hour. The van would not move. We went through five vans and crossed hundreds of thousands of miles from Seattle, Washington to Buffalo, New York, even going back to Houston a few times.

In October 1986, Teresa and I attended a World Series party. I remember retreating to a room alone, depressed that the Mets were about to be beaten by the Red Sox. Then came the Bill Buckner, "behind the bag" play and the Mets won. Celebrating afterwards, I met a man named John Allen. He was and still is obsessed with my picture "The Shell". Mr. Allen asked me, "What possessed you to take this shot?" But more important, he approached me because I had an awesome picture called "Homecoming". He told me that he and his partner, Mark Nichols, a banker, would possibly be interested in investing in a poster. On Halloween, I went to visit Mark, who was in a clown costume. I made my presentation. Mark became an investor in my work, and perhaps, a brother I never had.

"Homecoming"

On October 3rd, 1988, Teresa gave birth to a little sister for Chris, Leanne Marie. The following April, we moved from the frigid condo to a home in breathtaking Roxborough. Here I began to shoot, and our first snowy winter there, I came up with "Winter On The Rox". As I built up my Colorado inventory with shots like "Homecoming" and "A Breath Away From Heaven", we began doing lots of mountain shows. In the fall of 1992, while having an exhibit at the Town Hall Art Center in Littleton, I was standing outside during intermission with Lou Malandra, the director. We both noticed that Kerek's on the corner of West Main and Nevada was FOR LEASE. Lou quickly talked me into going for it and renting the place. This gift shop was actually the first store where I hung pictures in Colorado. On November 23rd, 1992 we opened our first gallery, 2509 West Main St. in downtown Littleton. Very soon I said to myself, "It's feels so good to leave at night and just turn off the light switch, instead of tearing down a booth." As we began to release new images, I started a tradition where the first piece exhibited to the public became a #3, keeping #1 and #2 available to us or family. This has continued to this very day, and the #3 is considered the most valuable piece in the edition.

In 1993, we met a couple at the Breckenridge show, who invited us to come stay a week at their home in Bermuda. Of course, we accepted, leaving Chris and Leanne with some friends. Invigorated by this adventure, trips followed to Greece, Africa and Hudson Bay, Canada to photograph the great polar bears. In the summer of 1996, Teresa informed me that once again, she was pregnant. So on March 19th, 1997, one day before Chris' birthday, Nicole (Nikki) Lynn was born. We were blessed with our third child. Mark "Sitting Crow" Nichols became her godfather, despite being a Red Sox fan. For the next ten years, we continued to do art shows, even though, we had the gallery.

In 2003, I published my first coffee table book, "Last Signs of the Frontier", a black and white collection of old signs, Colorado Roadside Nostalgia. In September of 2004, we bravely released two new books, "Early Signs of Enchantment" (A New Mexico version of the first) and "The Blue Bubble Lady" a children's magical story.

Saturday, September 25th, we had finished a Bubble Lady day at the gallery, promoting the book. Leanne dressed up as her. We closed the gallery, went to dinner with who else, but Mark. We said our goodnights and went on our way home. I had the routine of going for a night time walk, either with my huskie, Koshari, or sometimes alone. This night I went alone, while Teresa stayed home and watched Saturday Night Live. She fell asleep and was awakened hours later, by a call from Swedish Hospital. "Mrs. Marquez, your husband's been in a motorcycle accident, we need for you to come down here". She soon found out that I had been hit by an out of control motorcyclist, who fled the scene, but was later caught hiding, in the back seat of a parked car. I had a lot of surgeries, my hip; specifically the femur was the worst injury. A broken left knee and right ankle were others. To add to the misery, I had a traumatic brain injury. Teresa took aggressive action to make sure that I would get the best treatment possible, at the one and only Craig Hospital. Dark days followed, but Dr. Jim Berry kept telling me to follow the light. A lot of physical and occupational therapy filled my days. I had a goal to be home at Thanksgiving. The expert staff at Craig continued their efforts to help me learn to walk again. Beating the odds, I was with my family on this wonderful holiday. The next day – Black Friday – I sat in my wheel chair, back at the gallery, greeting my customers at Littleton's Candlelight Walk. Trips to Hawaii and China followed in 2005, as my legs began to function almost like before.

On July 6th of 2006, we were getting ready to head to Steamboat for a show we rarely missed. I received a phone call from the Grand Strand Hospital in North Myrtle Beach. Mom had a stroke and did not make it. Of course, we cancelled the show and made quick arrangements. Nikki flew with Teresa and I, while Chris and Leanne drove Teresa's Sebring across the country. Mom was 84; very stubbornly independent and so lived alone, since Dad died 24 years earlier. Her favorite thing to say to people when asked how are you? Her answer, most of the time was "great and grateful". So many people loved her. At her funeral, as per her request, we played "Amazing Grace" by Judy Collins. We wound up getting a quick rental of her condo, and proceeded back to our life in Colorado.

"A Breath Away From Heaven"

I had to put the final touches on our soon to be released new book of Colorado classics. Looking for a name for this feel good book, why not "Colorado: A Breath Away From Heaven", and – I decided to use the sold out edition photo for the cover shot. We had a Thanksgiving weekend delivery of the book. The release of this coffee table book for the holidays spinned us into our biggest month ever. On the first Saturday of December, a customer came in the gallery and said to us "I saw your article in the paper this morning, the Rocky Mountain News." I ran across the street and picked up a copy. Getting back inside, Teresa and I opened the paper, found the entertainment section and there in the column "Colorado's Best Bet for 2006" was "A Breath Away………." I was dumbfounded, caught between speechless and wanting to scream with utter happiness. What an honor. Thank you, Patty Thorn! A monumental moment in my career. Finally, the Littleton we had worked so hard to build over the years was beginning to click. A good feeling; however it did not last.

Many of the buildings on Main Street were beginning to sell for ridiculously high prices. This included my building. The new landlord gave us a rent increase more than triple what we had been paying. After 14 ½ years, it was time to say goodbye to our wonderful downtown. As we began to look for a new location, rents were rising everywhere. We found a place in upscale Cherry Creek, that was nearly $4,000 a month, which was less than what our Littleton landlord had wanted. I must say our excitement about locating in Cherry Creek was bigger than our business and common sense. We signed a three-year lease. Being so close to Josephine St., we were out of the main traffic flow. We had a great opening from our die-hard collectors followed by a very disappointing first eight months. In early 2008, business picked up with big dollar sales and the high rent seemed doable. A trip to Jordan and Israel with Chris, in early April gave me the material I needed to complete my 15 year collection of overseas images for the book, I'm so proud of, "Dreams That Last Forever", using my Prague bridge shot on the cover. As the book was being released, the economy tanked in October. Gallery traffic all but died. Leanne gave birth to Jude Jackson Marquez on June 4, 2009 and Teresa and I became proud grandparents. Somehow we toughed it through the Christmas season and 2009, with very few highlights. For the first year since 1992 there was not an overseas trip. 2010 was a struggle and the year ended with Teresa learning she had breast cancer. She began chemo treatments.

A few days before Easter weekend, I left alone, to do the St. George Arts Festival in Utah. Stopped in Monument Valley on the way there and shot a beautiful sunset, which I just recently released, called "Until Tomorrow". I was not feeling my best, but proceeded on to Zion where grey clouds dominated the sky. However, I took a real invigorating hike on one of the trails, but afterwards was feeling a bit wiped out. The show turned out to be significantly down from previous years. Despairingly I headed back to Denver, trying to get home for Easter dinner with the family. I made it, 660 miles later. Monday passed with the usual chores. On Tuesday, life changed. I woke up vomiting, called Doctor Von Rueden, my Kaiser Doc, who told me to go to the Swedish Emergency room. But Teresa called in the paramedics first and I was taken by ambulance to the hospital.

Not much do I remember about the time there. I had three stomach surgeries in 2 weeks for a bowel obstruction. The tough part followed. I was having some really funky dreams; I think it's called dementia. Apparently I had developed ARDS, Acute Respiratory Distress Syndrome, with a 70% mortality rate. The doctors induced a coma to try and stabilize me. This lasted about six weeks. One of the surgeons told Teresa "We've done all we can do." That day, Deacon Chet from St. Francis Cabrini, David Jarbo, a pastor from The Gathering at Roxborough and Mark Nichols, now a Shaman healer, all came and prayed for me. My family was called in to say their goodbyes. I can't imagine what they were going through. Teresa was continuing to undergo chemo, as I lay on my deathbed. That night something changed and I began to show signs of improvement. The doctors slowly brought me out of the coma and I began nearly a 3 month recovery and rehab. I could not talk for weeks because of a trachea down my throat. Still, I continued having the strangest dreams. In June, I was transferred to Cherrelyn Health Care Center in Littleton. I spent a couple of months there in rehab, learning once again to walk. At one point in July, Teresa had her last chemo treatment and was so sick, I didn't see her for a couple of weeks. I spent my evenings watching Rockies baseball, either with my friends Bob & Karen, or making my nightly calls to my bud, Kramer, to discuss the outcome. I eventually learned from Teresa that we had closed our gallery in Cherry Creek. In mid August I was released just before my 59th birthday. Some of our long time customers were encouraging us to return to Littleton. Teresa finally finished her radiation treatments and her beautiful hair started its journey back. Her most recent mammogram was clear. Thank God!

One of Littleton's better landlords, Rick Acres, went out of his way to find me a place back in Littleton. It felt good to be back. On November 18th, 2010, we reopened at the west end of Main St. We had a great interview on Channel 9 News with Gary Shapiro and received a nice series of articles written by my long time colleague, Sonia Ellingboe. We struggled through 2011 with the weak economy. Early summer, I was getting more stomach pain and a large lump was protruding from my abdomen. My friends, neighbors, printers and designers extraordinare, Bill and Jennie Heagle urged me to get it checked out. I went to the emergency room and the surgeon told me I had a massive incisional hernia, but I needed to see a Kaiser surgeon and then schedule an appointment from there. So in late July, I went back under the knife again to repair my entire stomach wall with mesh. It's been a tough recovery, but I've been working out to the best of my ability, 4 to 5 days a week and feel a lot better. On December 1st of 2011, we decided we needed a change of location. The west end of Littleton was not getting the job done. Our lease would end on Dec. 31st.

Being a person of increasingly strong faith, I believed that something good would happen before Christmas. At the recommendation of Father Sean and my friends at St. Francis Cabrini, I began to visit the adoration chapel almost daily. A couple of possibilities arose in the first week of the month. It was tricky, trying to work the retail end of the business while dealing with relocating. By the 15th of December both deals fell through, and I began to worry. Once, my friend Dr. Mitch told me "if you're worried, pray, and if you've prayed, don't worry". It was the morning of Dec. 23rd. We had begun to move some things home and others to our storage unit. That afternoon, Art Scape publisher, Chuck Whitely stopped by to pick out a gift. As he was leaving, he said he had an idea and would get back to me. On December 24, Christmas Eve, at about 1:00pm, the gallery phone rang. It was Jack Lima at the Native American Gallery in Denver. He said he was the landlord for the former Camera Obscura Gallery. Hal Gould, legendary photographer, who had been in the spot for 45 years, had retired and they were looking to bring in another photographer. They heard I was looking, and from what Chuck had told them, I was the one. We met the Monday after a nice Christmas, and on Thursday came to terms with Jack and his wife, Robin.

In two days, we set a new course and moved everything from Littleton to Denver, 1307 Bannock Street, across from the Byers Evans House Museum, the Denver Art Museum and the Clyfford Still Museum. Next door to me is my new friend, Mark Anthony King and his gallery, The Muse. Who could ask for better company? On January 27, 2012 we opened our doors in the Museum District of Denver's Golden Triangle. On May 15th of this year, as I prepare to release this book, Teresa and I celebrated 30 year of marriage.